WEIRD HOMES

Weird Homes Tour™ Presents

WEIRD HOMES

THE PEOPLE AND PLACES THAT KEEP AUSTIN STRANGELY WONDERFUL

DAVID J. NEFF AND CHELLE NEFF

PHOTOGRAPHS BY THANIN VIRIYAKI

Skyhorse Publishing

Skyhorse Publishing books may be purchased in bulk at special discounts for sales promotion, corporate gifts, fund-raising, or educational purposes. Special editions can also be created to specifications. For details, contact the Special Sales Department, Skyhorse Publishing, 307 West 36th Street, 11th Floor, New York, NY 10018 or info@skyhorsepublishing.com.

Skyhorse® and Skyhorse Publishing® are registered trademarks of Skyhorse Publishing, Inc.®, a Delaware corporation.

Visit our website at www.skyhorsepublishing.com.

10 9 8 7 6 5 4 3 2 1

Library of Congress Cataloging-in-Publication Data

Names: Neff, David J., 1977- author.
Title: Weird homes : the people and places that keep Austin strangely
   wonderful / David J. Neff and Chelle Neff.
Other titles: Weird Homes Tour presents Weird homes
Description: New York : Skyhorse Publishing, 2018.
Identifiers: LCCN 2017050972| ISBN 9781510723603 (hardcover : alk. paper) |
   ISBN 9781510723634 (Ebook)
Subjects: LCSH: Fantastic architecture--Texas--Austin. | Architecture,
   Domestic--Texas--Austin--Themes, motives. | Austin (Tex.)--Buildings,
   structures, etc.
Classification: LCC NA209.5 .N44 2018 | DDC 728.09764/31--dc23 LC record
available at https://lccn.loc.gov/2017050972
Cover design by Daniel Brount
Cover photograph by Thanin Viriyaki

Paperback ISBN: 978-1-5107-5922-0
Hardcover ISBN: 978-1-5107-2360-3
Ebook ISBN: 978-1-5107-2363-4

Printed in China

This book is dedicated to my mom, dad, and sister, who have always encouraged me to do my own thing, ever since I was eight years old. This book is dedicated to my wife, and founder of Weird Homes Tour, Chelle Neff. She is the most beautiful, intelligent, funny entrepreneur I have ever met. This book is dedicated to our amazing Weird Homes owners, who constantly surprise and delight us and our community with their art. And finally, because we are a community-minded, mission-driven company, this book is dedicated to all the affordable housing groups/nonprofits we invest in. Keep changing people's lives for the better. It's an honor to invest in you.

—David

Contents

Mobile Loaves & Fishes was already an Austin treasure. But then its 27-acre master-planned community called Community First! Village, providing affordable and sustainable housing to the chronically homeless in Austin, took shape. Now the nonprofit is a perfect fit for our tour, too.

Featuring an ark in the backyard and bright, whimsical decorations, this East Austin abode is home to Florence Ponziano who, for decades, has cared for neighborhood children. Her Comfort House is a safe and nurturing place for all who visit it.

We brought the Weird Homes Tour to Houston in October 2016 and the city welcomed us with open arms. From Tejano band La Mafia's former abode to artist Bonnie Blue's famous art house, take a sneak peek at our time in H-town.

Help us honor these homes and shine a spotlight on other homeowners who capture adventure, inspiration, and passion within their dwellings.

WHY SO WEIRD?

As the co-founders of the Weird Homes Tour in Austin, Texas, we've been privileged to see first-hand what makes our city so weird, whimsical, and wonderful. The tour has showcased homes in all their glorious eccentricity for thousands of people who have gone on the tour since 2014. With this book, we invite you to take your own virtual tour. Go behind the scenes to meet fabulous people and gawk at the inspired places that have made the tour such a success.

Austin has always been a hub of creativity, energy, art, and weirdness. It's full of artistic people who would rather be pirates than join the Navy. But Austin is rapidly changing. And, although we are proud of our growth, we want to fiercely guard what makes Austin unique.

Some of the homes we feature here have already changed hands. For a few, the owners simply moved on. For others, rising property taxes and

other hardships have forced these artists and visionaries to sell the homes they so passionately cultivated. Keeping Austin strangely wonderful is one of the goals we had in founding the Weird Homes Tour, and preserving that strangeness is why we fought to make this book a reality.

An Inside Look at Homes with Souls

Within these pages, thanks to the help of renowned Texas photographer Thanin Viriyaki, we've captured the original homes on our tour. Every stained glass window, pop-culture tchotchke, work of outsider art, and piece of junk-turned-treasure represents a dream, memory, or other cherished part of these homeowners' lives. We are forever grateful to them for opening their hearts, their souls, and their homes to us and to the thousands who have been able to explore these homes firsthand on the tour.

Casa Neverlandia, for example, is a fantastical place which looks like the set of a Tim Burton film. It has a whimsical rainbow exterior, secret passages, and an elevated footbridge. In the Johnson/Chronister Manor, you'll find stained glass, hidden spiral staircases, and a belfry with a bat. At the home of Austin's "Queen of the Weird," you'll see Betty Boop figurines, tin toys, and paintings of monkeys, all from her eclectic childhood.

Another goal we had when we started the Weird Homes Tour was, quite simply, to give back. We created a social impact startup that cares about people, the planet, and making a profit in order to give back. In our first three years in Austin, we've been able to invest in both Foundation Communities and Caritas. With our help and the help of others in the Austin area, Foundation

Communities provides affordable, attractive homes and free on-site support services for thousands of families. And, for Caritas, proceeds from our tour's ticket sales have helped furnish new homes for people who were living on the streets or provide emergency rent and utility assistance for families, helping them avoid eviction.

While this book features Austin, we've already expanded the Weird Homes Tour to Houston. We've set our sights on New Orleans and, perhaps, Portland, Detroit, and San Francisco after that. In each of these great cities, we want to honor, celebrate, and preserve the subculture by recognizing what makes it eccentric, lovable, and irreplaceable.

Our hope is that, through this book, you will take away design, architecture, and art tips and tricks to add flair to your own everyday spaces. We guarantee there is inspiration inside these pages. In the process, you're certain to come away with a true appreciation for what these artists have done to transform their own spaces.

CHAPTER ONE
CASA NEVERLANDIA

Secret passages, an elevated footbridge, fire poles, and a hidden concert stage—as well as rainwater collection tanks and solar panels—are among the surprises in this jewel, located in the south Austin Bouldin Creek neighborhood.

Casa Neverlandia is a magnificent home created and constantly re-imagined by artist James Talbot, along with his friends and family, since 1979. Talbot is an artist who creates fine art in 3-D, including work in mosaics, glass, metals, beads, plastics, and ceramics, all of which is reflected in the inventive play-scape of his home.

"I'm intrigued about what makes a place or thing magical," says Talbot, "and I'm learning to identify and use different elements of this hidden domain."

Ropes, spires, an observation tower, and crystals give Casa Neverlandia the feel of a wizard's lair. And, rumor has it, an outdoor shower—perched on the second floor—is being installed, to add a bit more organic flair. Perhaps weirdest of all in our era of climate-controlled comfort: Casa Neverlandia has no air conditioning or heating.

A Pantheistic, Pan-Cultural World

As owner and artist of Neverland Designs, Talbot is a hands-on artist, designer, and builder comfortable with both small- and large-scale media, in both public and private settings. He works with architects, artists, landscapers, and contractors.

Casa Neverlandia itself draws inspiration from many places. The international feel of this house springs from Talbot's childhood and his extensive travels. Raised in a military family, Talbot had lived on five continents by the time he reached college and, to date, has lived in or visited thirty-three countries.

"I live in a pantheistic, pan-cultural world in which things have a life of their own—they express deeper meaning and are not simply what they seem. Places I've lived—Spain, Morocco, Turkey, England, Venezuela, the Texas Hill Country—have profoundly influenced me (some at a preverbal level), their cultural biases intermingling freely inside me."

"Nature provides more springboards: textures, color gradations, cloudscapes, layered panoramas, smoke, waterways, the more colorful animals and their surface patterns (tropical fish and butterflies are favorites), stone, stalactites, flowers, bones."

13

CHAPTER TWO
THE EARTHBAG HOUSE

Tucked away behind the charming Austin restaurant Hillside Farmacy is a structure that some might say appears to be more hive than home. But home it is: an earthbag home, to be precise.

The building uses burlap to hold dirt that very closely resembles adobe. These earthbags are filled from the top of the wall, scoop by scoop, with locally sourced dirt. No metric tons of bricks and all the water it takes to make them. No fiberglass and the chemicals it takes to make those, either. These homes are notable due to their low cost in materials, low skill in building required, outstanding strength, and resistance to hurricanes, tornadoes, earthquakes, fire, and termites.

Environmentalist, humanitarian, and engineer Nader Khalili is credited with developing the idea of earthbag structures more than fifty years ago. His organization, the California Institute of Earth Architecture (CalEarth), works with the United Nations and other organizations around the globe to help rebuild communities facing a housing crisis. Most recently, these structures have been built to help provide housing to refugees in Iran, Haiti earthquake survivors, and Pakistan earthquake refugees.[1]

1   California Institute of Earth Architecture. "The Global Impact of Superadobe." Accessed December 2, 2019. https://www.calearth.org/relief-initiatives.

A True Labor of Love . . . and Endurance

Back home in Texas, this particular earthbag home was built with love, sweat, and tears by its amazing and dedicated owner, Bill Rosenthal, natural building expert Thea Bryant, and a few helpers. The 2-bedroom, 1.5 bathroom, 750-square-foot home was completed after 4,000 hours over the span of four years.[2]

"Building an earthbag house was an intense goal for me . . . and a big part of the magic behind our successful team was definitely Bill's adventurous building spirit," Bryant says. "He has such a different way of viewing the building industry and so much knowledge that when he showed interest in building an earthbag, I was really excited to know that I'd have someone to lend a helping hand on this big journey I was going to attempt to do . . . no matter what."[3]

2   Breaux, Adrienne. "Urban Nomads." Tribeza, September 29, 2013. https://issuu.com/tribeza/docs/october_tribeza2013.

3   Earthbag House. "Our Story." Accessed February 20, 2017. http://www.earthbaghouse.com/Ourstory.html.

While earthbag homes are eco-friendly and sustainable, they can also be a bit messy to perfect.

"We hauled sixty-five gallons [of local clay] down the riverbed, up a thirty-foot bank, and across a field. We were exhausted," Bryant remembers. "I experimented with that clay for three months: drying it, pulverizing, trying to dissolve it. All along I was getting to understand the material more and more. It's so interesting how you can play with a material until you finally get to a point where you just 'know' it so well."

By the time the home was opened as part of the Weird Homes Tour, Bryant was living there with her four children. Every nook and cranny of the cornerless house was packed with love—colorful blankets, stuffed animals, and living necessities. But, even so, the domed space seems reminiscent of Doctor Who's telephone box: bigger on the inside. The breathtaking focal point? The main skylighted dome spiraling over the kitchen.

Chapter Three
Under the Sea

Nestled in the classic Austin weirdness zone of the 78704 lies this home dedicated to bold, bright colors and even bolder, brighter ideas. From the moment we saw the art car pulling into the driveway we knew this home was destined for the Weird Homes Tour. This complete work of art is home to Lois Goodman, who's been there more than 20 years, working on the home.

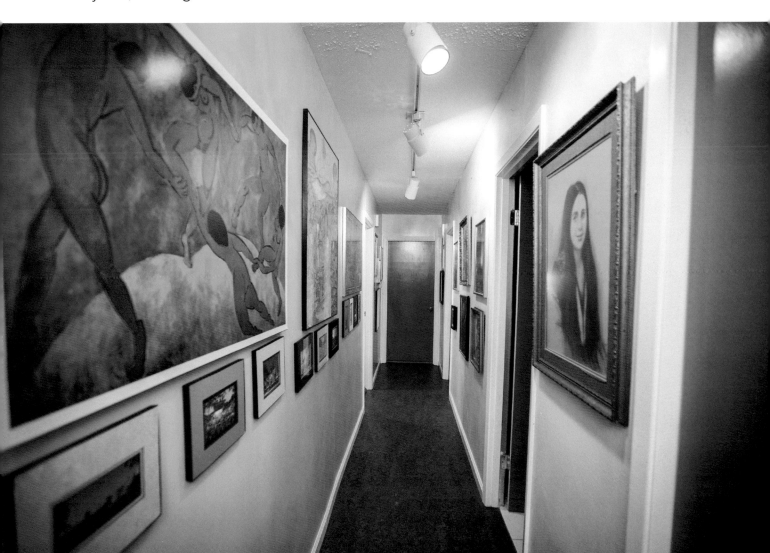

The interior has a multitude of collections and a uniquely lit bathroom with 109 dichroic glass tiles. Salt and pepper shakers, miniature shoes, and matches are all part of the collections. When Goodman moved into the home in 1993, she immediately painted all the walls white in order to conform to what she thought would be "normal." Decades later, there are at least 26 different colors used throughout the exterior and interior.[4]

4   McDonald, Kelli. "Exclusive Preview: Austin Weird Homes Tour 2015." *The Austinot*, May 12, 2015. http://austinot.com/weird-homes-tour-2015.

What Lies Beneath

While the interior is spectacular, it's the backyard that gives the home its aquatic name.

"I created a 'rock' star rock garden, a swing with a chandelier, and a fence with an undersea mural on the exterior," says Goodman. That mural includes a stingray, orcas, a sea lion, and Lois herself . . . as a mermaid. But the true reason she's featured in the mural isn't self-gratification. Her nineteen-year-old cats, Dodo and Delilah, are buried just below the mermaid so that she can forever keep them company.[5]

5   Kelso, John. "Austinite keeps it weird with art car, house."
    Austin American-Statesman, September 23, 2016.
    https://www.statesman.com/news/20160923/kelso-austinite-keeps-
    it-weird-with-art-car-house.

But let's get back to that art car, for which Goodman is best known. While her beloved 1995 Honda Accord wagon named "Carsmos" is arguably the most recognized car in Austin, it wasn't her first attempt at an art car. In fact, Carsmos is a fourth generation creation of Goodman's. The planets on the roof of the car were created by a local metal worker whose wife teaches astronomy. Much of the rest of the car's charm—including numerous figurines—is courtesy of what Goodman considers one of her best talents.

"I'm the gluer," she once told the *Austin American-Statesman's* John Kelso. "I have a vision, and I can glue. That's the extent of my abilities."[6]

Alas, Carsmos is retirement-ready and Goodman is in the process of finding the beloved car a new, permanent home. But don't fret. Her current car is an art car, too. And "Mermania" is true to its name, spreading her mermaid love (that once grew only in Goodman's back yard) across the entire city.

6   Kelso, John. "Austinite keeps it weird with art car, house." *Austin American-Statesman*, September 23, 2016.
    https://www.statesman.com/news/20160923/kelso-austinite-keeps-it-weird-with-art-car-house.

Chapter Four
The Collectors

If you assumed the owner of Austin's iconic South Congress vintage store Uncommon Objects would have a weird home, you would be 100% correct. This house in Travis Heights is a collection of collections, a virtual treasure trove of fascination, a mecca of wonder.

Steve Wiman has owned the home for nearly a quarter of a century and, just like his store, it has become packed with beautifully strange things. As you enter the home, you are greeted by a wall of thirty years of Christmas ornaments handmade by friends. When *The Austinot's* Kelly McDonald asked Wiman whether a particular ornament stood out to him, he took a moment and showed her a single, broken leaf that had been sewn back up and stitched with the words "On the Mend." This particular ornament was part of a good health theme the year his wife suffered from a stroke.[7]

7   McDonald, Kelli. "Peek Inside 6 Bizarre Homes from Austin Weird Homes Tour 2016."
    The Austinot, May 10, 2016. http://austinot.com/weird-homes-tour-2016.

From there, you're off to explore hidden gems both large and small around every corner, including collections of seeds, baseballs, cowboy boots, dice, art, and who knows what else. Every cabinet, and every shelf, is filled with life's jewels waiting to be discovered, each one with its own story.

There Is No Object So Foul

What brought Wiman to this place of creating and collecting uncommon treasures? The assemblage artist had a proper Texan upbringing as a graduate of the University of North Texas and attendee of graduate art school at the University of Texas. He credits studying color and composition through painting for giving him his aesthetic foundation.

"Years ago, I encountered a quotation credited to Ralph Waldo Emerson that resonated with me," Wiman reflects. "Emerson said, 'There is no object so foul that an intense light will not render beautiful.' This truth has inspired and illuminated my art-making. Finding beauty in the mundane and shining a light on it is my mission as an artist."[8]

8   Webpage of Steve Winman. "About/Contact." Accessed December 2, 2019. https://cargocollective.com/stevewiman/About-Contact

Chapter Five
Riggins's Cabinet of Curiosity

When Cathy DeYoung and Michael Hayes bought their University Hills home, they had no idea it had an infamous past. Turns out it had been featured in the *Friday Night Lights* television series as the home of high school football hunk Tim Riggins. While the cult-hit series might not be with us anymore, Riggins's house has found a new life as a Cabinet of Curiosities.

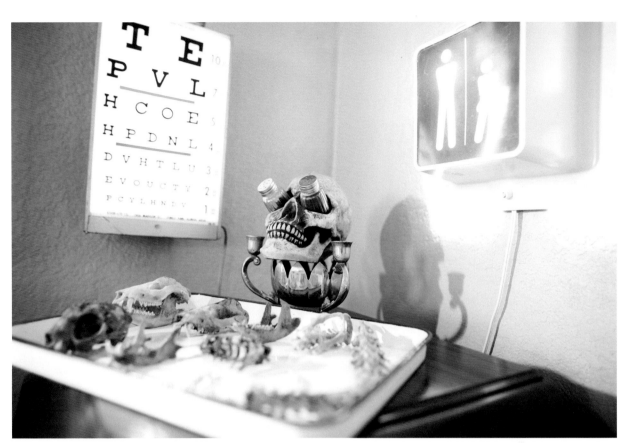

A police car hood attached to the ceiling, complete with working siren, greets visitors as they enter into a house bursting at the seams with macabre oddities. A WWII portable birthing/surgical table stands in for a credenza and a Victorian coffin dolly, complete with antique gynecological devices, acts as a coffee table.

The most comfortable chair in the house is a 1930's dental chair. Lamps are made from x-rays, silkworm cocoons, and a pink 1950's salon hairdryer. The guest bathroom is covered with blood spatter (it's fake, we were told). It also features a hollowed-out armadillo containing washcloths for guests, thoughtfully watched over by fifteen muskrat skulls and several grenades.

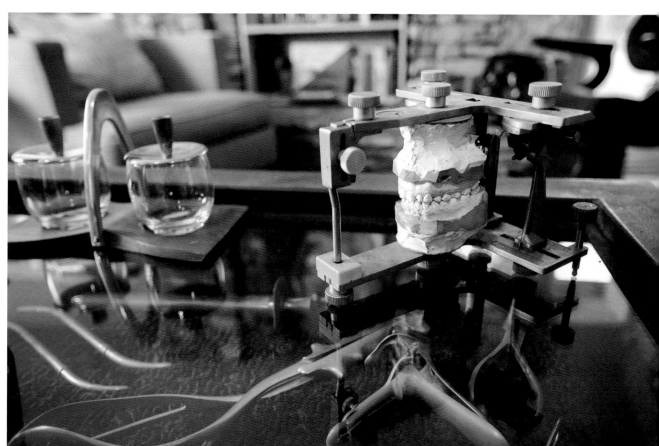

Creativity Is Not a Crime

While this menagerie may seem random, it all becomes clear once you get to know the homeowners. Hayes is an avid and eclectic artist, designer, and motorcycle enthusiast who built their backyard studio with his own two hands.

45

And then there's DeYoung.

As a student in Los Angeles, she honed her photography skills with local, state, and federal law enforcement agency task forces including narcotics, gangs, vice, and DUI. After graduation, she pursued photography in the entertainment industry, government and aerospace, and civil litigation.

Ten years later, DeYoung returned to her college-days roots and joined the crime lab. In just short of seven years, she investigated over 6,000 crime scenes, often in some of the most notorious neighborhoods in LA.[9] Rumor has it, she even inspired the *NCIS* character Abby Sciuto. For more about her life as a crime investigator, check out her book *Life in the Trenches: A Retrospective*, which offers a fun, sarcastic, and honest glimpse into the scenes hidden behind the police barrier tape.

This home has recently sold. RIP, Riggins's Cabinet of Curiosity.

9   Website of Catherine DeYoung. "Life in the Trenches Books." Accessed February 20, 2017. http://lifeinthetrenchesbook.com/.

CHAPTER SIX
BARTON HILLS ART OASIS

Metal artist Valerie Chaussonnet calls this Barton Hills treasure her home. In every sense, her house epitomizes the definition of art. Metal sculptures adorn every room, including a metal portrait of a famous Russian witch, Baba Yaga, that guards the library.

The house itself—which was once a French daycare/school—is an always-evolving work of art that Valerie hopes will never be complete. Whether it's the sky-painted ceiling, mosque-inspired doorway with matching cat door, closets that have become bookshelves, or bookshelves that have become closets, the house is always in a state of development. The whimsical furniture, from squared-circle (or is it circled-square?) chairs to a loveseat that looks like a plush Viking ship, are all one-of-a-kind creations, designed and built by Valerie's husband.

Beauty in Metal Things

Chaussonnet is an anthropologist, which has allowed her to develop a beautiful way of entwining culturally significant images. Early in her career, she traveled extensively as a team member for the Smithsonian's Arctic Studies Center.

"The project took me to European Russia, Alaska, and Siberia, and their museums had storage rooms full of the most extraordinary native art," she says. At the same time, she studied Sculpture and Art Furniture at the Corcoran Art School in D.C. and learned welding under Baltimore artist Donna Reinsel. Once she began working with metal, she felt she finally had an art language that could tie her love of native art and sculpture together.

"I like the weight and the look of thick steel because it appears industrial and indestructible," Chaussonnet says. "And then I love the chunks, pipes, and sheets used by apprentice welders and art metal students in class. Covered with practice welds, like so many scars, cut, rewelded for fun or work, they are tossed and ready to recycle again. Those long braids of welding beads made from hours of concentrated effort in patience, frustration, wonder, curiosity, bored resignation, or playful mastery, move me and inspire me as expressions of human labor."[10]

10 Website of Valerie Chaussonnet. "Bio." Accessed February 20, 2017. http://valeriechaussonnet.com/bio.html

CHAPTER SEVEN
BARBARA'S BIRDCAGE

In East Austin's Upper Boggy Creek, you will find the home of artist Barbara Irwin. Barbara is a found object artist who has made a career of transforming castaway items into unique works of art. In the process, she turned her house into a found object gallery, literally filled with works of art, from doll heads to bird cages to totems of power.

"When we learn to realize the uniqueness and beauty in everything, then we can understand that nothing is ever ordinary," Irwin says. Her home certainly reflects this conviction and she invites visitors to explore it with curiosity, to stretch their imaginations and see things in a new light. By doing this, she hopes to spread the joy, inspiring others to decorate their homes in a different way.

A Child's Sense of Wonder

During her lifetime, Irwin has tried her hand at being an interior designer, a department store buyer, a certified Montessori teacher, and an herbalist. She was even involved in building a forty-two-foot trimaran sailboat and sailing from Texas to Hawaii. Ever since her teenage years she has created collages, but it was not until she was in her forties that she actually considered putting art out into the world.

One of Irwin's favorite quotes comes from Rachel Carson's book *A Sense of Wonder*. It reads, "A child's world is fresh and new and beautiful, full of wonder and excitement. It is our misfortune that for most of us that clear-eyed vision, that true instinct for what is beautiful and awe-inspiring, is dimmed and even lost before we reach adulthood."

"Carson is talking very specifically in her book about wonder as it relates to the natural world, but my sense of wonder extends to almost all things," Irwin reflects. "That is the basis for my work. A rusty piece of metal on the side of the road is not just trash. It has its own inherent beauty and I notice that. I think about it, am in awe of it, and incorporate it into artwork so that other people also have the opportunity to see, to wonder, and to appreciate."[11]

11 Website of Barbara Irwin. "Statement." Accessed February 20, 2017. http://foundobjectart.com/statement.htm.

Chapter Eight
Rancho Burrito/Institute of Materials Interpretation

Is it a shipping container, a business, a farm, an experiment, a home? The answer: Yes, it is! This East Austin one-bedroom, one-bathroom, 280-square-foot home is, indeed, made from a steel shipping container. While these big metal objects are used to haul goods across the world, they can also make deceivingly cool homes.

During the original Weird Homes Tour, the container home was in the process of being completed. In the end, owner J. Zach Hollandsworth is using a high percentage of re-used materials to create the most environmentally friendly house in the city. Other features on his wish list: a productive farm, solar chimney, wood-burning hot tub (which is already in place), bees, chickens, and more.

"Eventually, I'll be off the grid, mostly passive, and producing enough food to eat or trade, all of my energy, and water, all on site, making me carbon negative (that is, using less carbon than I produce, through energy creation, carbon sequestering, and the use of reused materials)," he explains. "There's no reason why this weird couldn't become the new normal." When asked if Austin is becoming less weird, he said that the reason most houses look the same is that there are "rules" that say they should. He is hoping to change some of that.

Weird Is Normal

"Weird to me is normal," Hollandsworth says. "A nice thing about Austin is that, as I question and deviate from society's norms, people are supportive and excited to see an alternative lifestyle."

And although shipping container homes are weird when it comes to traditional housing, the trend is taking off in other areas. Like its cousin the earthbag home, shipping container homes are currently being used to house the homeless in Orange County, California; military personnel in Afghanistan and Iraq; backyard renters in Portland, Oregon; and students in Amsterdam, Netherlands.[12]

We're so inspired, we're even looking to do our own shipping container project in 2019.

---

12 Chow, Lorraine. "Love This!" *EcoWatch*, September 26, 2016. http://www.ecowatch.com/shipping-containr-homes-2012538184.html.

CHAPTER NINE
EPONYMOUS GARDEN

There is perhaps no better bridge to Austin's past—and to the weird oddities that have inhabited the city for decades—than this compound that includes an 1880s Eastlake-style Victorian and three 1930s craftsman bungalows. The private, fenced property filled with trees, flowers, herbs, and walking trails has many stories to tell. In its 135-year existence, it has been home to artists, entertainers, writers, philosophers . . . and circus performers.

When actors Lorne Loganbill and Sterling Price-McKinney acquired the property several years ago, they established it as a destination for vacation renters and special events. Under their careful vision, the property—best known as the historic McGown-Griffin House—became a unique tribute to its weird and wonderful past.

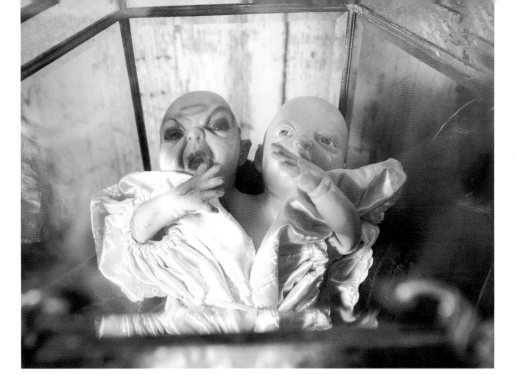

A Past Like No Other

What Loganbill and Price-McKinney could piece together is that the early occupants of the McGown-Griffin House included a menagerie of colorful personalities, among them a trustee of the German School, a prominent physician, and the builder of the Elisabet Ney studio. More recently, owners and inhabitants can be connected to the beloved Austin "sideshows" *Esther's Follies* and *Greater Tuna*.[13] Starting with the state senator thought to have built the house in the 1880s, residents and guests have run the gamut from the ridiculous to the sublime.

---

13 The Eponymous Gardener. "Suspend Time With Us at Eponymous Garden." Accessed February 20, 2017. https://eponymousgarden.wordpress.com/2013/10/09/suspend-time-with-us-at-eponymous-garden/.

Loganbill and Price-McKinney decided to honor the compound's past by maintaining much of the home's historic charm inside the main house. At the same time, they reserved the backyard for a more irreverent purpose: a circus sideshow museum. A series of sheds along the perimeter of the property house shrines to the weird and wonderful. A small shed served as a shrine honoring Mother Mary. The larger structure included countless circus and sideshow memorabilia that had to be seen to be believed.

Alas, the couple has since sold the home and has moved to Amarillo, taking the two-headed baby, bottles of snake oil, and other sideshow oddities with them. Is it the end of the Eponymous Garden saga? Only time will tell. One thing is certain, though: We are grateful to have captured its magic when we did.

CHAPTER TEN
SHARON'S HOUSE

With an unassuming name like "Sharon's House," how weird could this place be? See for yourself. Owner Sharon Smith is a well-known Austin Community College professor and ceramic artist whose work has won numerous accolades, including an artist-in-residence position at the Resen Ceramic Colony in Macedonia in 1997 and a National Endowment for the Arts Fellowship Award in Crafts in 1995. She also holds a Master of Arts in Raku Ceramics from the University of Dallas in Irving, Texas.

Smith is a cherished teacher and mentor to many, including fellow Weird Homes Tour homeowner James Talbot of Casa Neverlandia. Throughout her career, Smith has taught ceramics, drawing, fabrics, Raku handbuilding and firing, and art history at the university level.

Shrine After Shrine

Now, when's she not teaching ceramics at the local community college, Smith is spending time in her life's work, her weird home. Every room is decorated with a variety of shrines and other artifacts based on numerous religions and life events from her years on this planet.

"When I entered, I saw that the house was alive and breathing with folk art," says Kelly McDonald of *The Austinot*, who admits the home is so captivating that, a few months after she first visited, she was still thinking about it. "When you walk in the door, you're greeted by shrines and tables covered in art from floor to ceiling. A clear pathway winding throughout the house takes you on a tour that requires you to stay on the route and appreciate the eclectic sights around you."[14]

14 McDonald, Kelli. "One of Austin's Weirdest Homes: Sharon's Folk Art House." *The Austinot*, September 21, 2015. http://austinot.com/sharons-folk-art-house-austin.

Like so many other Weird Homes Tour homeowners, Smith traveled the world beginning in her early 20s and started collecting art pieces along the way. Her worldwide adventures began in Europe as she traveled across Germany, Switzerland, Spain, and England. Some of her most cherished pieces, though, include South American and Mexican religious folk art. She also loves objects that may seem, to others, broken, destroyed, or useless. These often include broken pottery from the local folk art store, a lost button, or a single earring from an estate sale.

101

Some of these smaller items have found new life glued into mosaics as doorway or even ceiling embellishments. The others find their places among Smith's own ceramics and even eclectic, dusty pieces dropped off in front of her home, perhaps by a neighbor or a student who knows even the most broken or forgotten art—as long as it has a story to tell—will find its place in Smith's home.

Chapter Eleven
The Johnson-Chronister Manor

Who said weird can't be elegant? At the top of a hill in the hills of West Austin, there's a secretive English manor-inspired home filled with stained glass, covert closets, hidden spiral staircases, and even a belfry. Visitors to the home are often most impressed by the "green man face" fireplace and the mythical creatures etched into stained glass doors.

Take a look around the Johnson-Chronister Manor and you'll feel whisked back in time. But assuming the gothic, medieval manor is devoid of modern touches, however, would be a huge mistake.

The owners happen to be award-winning architect Elliot Johnson, who designed it, and his amazing artist wife, Lisa Chronister. The two set out to create a storybook effect with ultramodern efficiencies. The result is an eco-conscious "castle" that includes a photovoltaic solar system, a thermal chimney for natural cooling, water-conserving plumbing, a tight thermal envelope, and almost all salvaged interior materials.

A Cupola Old World Touches

Nearly every aspect of the home is an experiment in eco-conscious living, from the cast earth walls to the deck and fence made from cedar trees reclaimed onsite. The passive solar technique used in the home is called a cupola and is based on an ancient concept of air movement that Johnson is helping to resurrect with this and other homes he has built. These efforts have earned the home several architectural and green building awards.

The couple admits part of the inspiration of the home comes from their love of J.R.R. Tolkien's stories, which wouldn't surprise visitors in the least. While the "bones" of the house are truly modern and innovative, much of the artwork and salvaged materials used to decorate it are fantastically Old World. A copper sink from Mexico, antique French doors from Argentina, and stained glass windows constructed by Lisa herself combine to give the home a grandness far beyond its recent birthdate.

"We often get asked how old our home is," Elliot told *Mother Earth Living*. "We're glad that it looks older. That was our goal."[15]

15 DeBacker, Gina. "Minding the Manor: A Cast Earth Home in Texas." *Mother Earth Living*, November/December 2008. http://www.motherearthliving.com/Green-Homes/Cast-Earth-English-Manor

Chapter Twelve
The Dumpster Project

In stark contrast to the more grandiose homes on the tour is the ultimate homage to downsizing. This home doesn't just look like a dumpster, it *is* a dumpster. It was also home for an entire year to Huston-Tillotson University Professor Jeff Wilson, aka Professor Dumpster.

Don't assume Wilson was reduced to living in a dumpster due to the poor living wages of an educator. Rather, the temporary living arrangement was part of an ongoing experiment called The Dumpster Project, which aimed to serve as a re-imagining of home, a portable learning initiative, and a sustainability conversation. With a team of students, experts, and colleagues, Wilson slowly transformed the 33-square-foot trash receptacle from a barely habitable used garbage container to a sustainable house and interactive teaching lab.

A Dumpster with All the Perks

What does home look like in a world of 10 billion people? How do we equip current and future generations with the tools they need for sustainable living practices? These are the questions Wilson and his students and colleagues set off to answer with The Dumpster Project.

By the time the dumpster was open to the Weird Homes Tour, it had become (dare we say?) quite the comfortable and stylish living space. Wilson and Huston-Tillotson University's Green Is the New Black (GITNB) student organization had renovated the dumpster to include a false floor "basement" that stores cooking equipment, bedding and clothing, an improved roof, solar lighting, bug repellant systems, an online weather data station, and (perhaps most important to a dumpster dwelling in the heart of Texas) an air-conditioning unit.

While you might assume the dumpster lifestyle is a lonely existence (hardly room for one visitor, much less a cocktail party), the experiment in sustainability turned up some surprising results when it comes to social behavior and communal living.

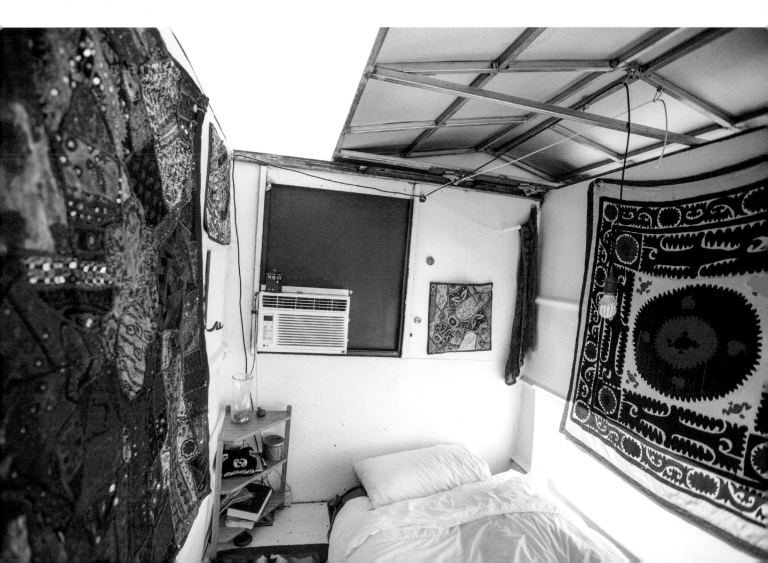

"I almost feel like East Austin [became] my home and backyard," Wilson told the *Atlantic*. "I know I have met a much wider circle of people just from going to laundromats and wandering around outside of the dumpster when I would've been in there if I had a large flat screen and a La-Z-Boy."[16]

Although Wilson's time of calling the dumpster home has passed, it continues to house curious educators and artists. In fact, individuals can apply for a chance to spend up to five nights in the dumpster through The Dumpster Project's Residency Program.

16 Hamblin, James. "Living Simply in a Dumpster." *The Atlantic*, September 11, 2014. http://www.theatlantic.com/health/archive/2014/09/the-simple-life-in-a-dumpster/379947/.

Chapter Thirteen
The Home of Austin's Queen of the Weird

Whimsical and perverse. It would be odd to see these two words used together to describe a home's decor if the homeowner weren't Aralyn Hughes. The indelible icon was once called the "Queen of the Weird in Austin" by a CBS national news program, a title she embraces with pride.

It's difficult to pinpoint exactly what accomplishment Hughes is best known for among her fellow Austinites. Could it be her long-running one-woman autobiographical shows? Her "Keep Austin Weird" home that she owned for twenty-seven years near Enfield and MoPac? Her "Home Economics" art car (you know, the one with the bananas on top)? Maybe it's her top-selling book *Kid Me Not*, an anthology by child-free women from the 60s now in their sixties? Or, perhaps, it's the award-winning documentary featuring Hughes as a 60-something wannabe dominatrix, with music by Shakey Graves?

However you know her, you know Austin's Queen of the Weird is always good for a story, a laugh, and plenty of weirdness. So when Hughes decided to move to a shiny new apartment by Lady Bird Lake, the whole of Austin wondered, "Is that the end of the queen's reign?" Has she conformed to societal norms?

Thankfully, she had not.

What Does Nonconformity Look Like?

While Austin's downtown apartments tend to feel cookie-cutter, Aralyn's maintains her quirky charm. From the moment visitors enter, their senses are gleefully assaulted with brilliant, bright colors popping left and right and eclectic furniture calling out to be touched. This includes original tin toys from her childhood, dolls wearing tiny handmade dresses (that were made to match her own dresses as a kid), and her original tricycle from when she was five. Colorful paintings, many of which were painted by Hughes herself, adorn the walls.

"Don't forget to peek inside my closet!" Hughes would tell visitors on the Weird Homes Tour. Every inch of her unit is filled with colorful knickknacks and artwork, including those spaces the rest of us would rather hide from the world. What's more, every single one has a story, a story Hughes will gladly share with unabashed enthusiasm.

Chapter Fourteen
Flamingo Ranch

When we first set out on our Weird Homes Tour adventure, we knew we'd offer a great service to the public: unprecedented access behind the gates and beyond the front doors of Austin's most deliciously curious homes. But, after several years, we realized an even greater purpose. Without any premeditation on our part, we've become the historical documentarians and storytellers for these Austin treasures, some of which are already lost to us.

Flamingo Ranch is one such lost treasure.

This South Austin vacation home was described as warm and inviting, drenched in color, soul, and light. Set under majestic oak trees alongside Dawson Creek, the home created a private, charming, enchanting experience for all who visited it.

Flamingo Ranch was owned and curated by Stefanie Distefano, who now resides in the quaint and artsy town of Smithville, Texas. The ranch was where she taught art classes and exhibited her talents as a ceramic and mosaic artist. When Distefano first bought the home in 2003, it was a basic, beige blank slate. Over time, she transformed the space into an artist's wonderland.

139

What Is Lost and What Remains

The home itself was a cozy 420 square feet, with places to lounge and relax filling nearly every nook. The house was surrounded by a screened-in porch with both indoor and outdoor lounging and sleeping spaces, all inviting and unique. The shimmery kitchen was a must see: Its facade was the result of hours of gluing glitter and sequins.

After moving through the living area, featuring mosaic flooring (created by Distefano herself), pink furniture, and a tumbleweed chandelier, you reached the studio where Distefano created her ceramic and mosaic magic. Beyond the studio was a vast back-yard, perfect for parties. In fact, Distefano built a stage there for occasional concerts and performances.

Since being featured on the Weird Homes Tour, Flamingo Ranch was sold and the home was recently leveled. But, rest assured, her footprint as an artist remains in the mosaics she continues to create around the region. Perhaps her most famous piece is a sprawling mural welcoming visitors at the Austin Nature & Science Center. There's also a Mahatma Gandhi mural (seen and admired by Gandhi's grandson) adorning East First Grocery on E. Cesar Chavez, a kid-favorite signature flamingo mural at Patterson Park, and dozens of other mosaics commissioned by neighborhood associations, small businesses, individuals, and even the City of Austin itself.

Chapter Fifteen
The Freeman House

The Wooten Park area of Austin is a neighborhood with many secret treasures. The Freeman House is one of those secrets. If you live in the neighborhood, chances are you've driven by this place a hundred times and never spotted anything out of the ordinary. Behind the hand-built, six-foot limestone walls surrounding this hidden gem, however, lies a truly unique oasis.

This Mexican-inspired hacienda is the hidden artist's retreat of owners Darryl Freeman and his wife Cindy. In addition to Darryl's art studio, the compound is home to Cindy's private acupuncture practice. The studio and home are full of strange and original oil paintings (many of which are Darryl's pieces) and many unique treasures gathered in their over twenty years of travel and adventure together.

A Fleeting Moment of Light

"It is immensely satisfying to me to capture a beautiful moment in time on my canvas," Darryl explains. "Often it's outdoors where I am most inspired . . . Sometimes, it's just a fleeting moment of light that I preserve. My paintings express gratitude for moments that have lifted my spirits and pleased my senses. They serve as a history of my experience, reminding me of things I have seen, and how I see things."[17]

17 Art Connections Gallery. "Darryl Freeman." Accessed February 20, 2017. http://www.artconnectionsgallerybastrop.com/darryl-freeman.html.

While the lovely home ensconced in this oasis features an awe-inspiring assortment of Darryl's oil paintings and other works of art, some would say the backyard is a work of art unto itself. It's there you'll find a chicken yard, two koi ponds, an aviary, many tropical and native Texas plants, and a rain collection system that sustains it all.

CHAPTER SIXTEEN
KASITA

In case you're wondering, Professor Dumpster, aka Jeff Wilson of The Dumpster Project (chapter 12), has moved on from living in the trash. But while his new abode is more sleek and sophisticated, it's still on the micro end of the spectrum.

The Dumpster Project prompted Wilson to "dig deeper" on the issue of small living and to re-imagine what a comfortable home could be. The burning questions he set out to answer: What will affordable, urban housing of the future look like in a growing city like Austin? Can it be adaptable and efficient but also beautifully designed?

The answer he came up with is KASITA: a futuristic metal and glass housing unit measuring approximately 350 square feet, packed with smart technology and custom home furnishings. Wilson spent three years researching and developing this KASITA prototype and unveiled it at SXSW® Interactive, where it was awarded the 2016 SXSW Innovation Award in the Smart Cities category.

A Beautiful Solution

Wilson's vision for the unit expands far beyond this one prototype. Imagine entire communities made of these gorgeous smart homes in the near future. Designed to stack on underutilized plots of urban land, the units can fit where conventional housing developments do not.

"Urban housing is perhaps the single most important factor in facing the economic, environmental, and social challenges that face humanity today," said Wilson. "Every aspect of KASITA—from its high-tech prefabricated construction to its ability to set up quickly on discounted land—was designed to create both an amazing living experience and produce development and living costs that crush traditional site building in terms of affordability."[18]

18 KASITA press release. "Micro Prefab Housing Startup KASITA is Revolutionizing Attainable Urban Living." BusinessWire, March 16, 2016. https://www.businesswire.com/news/home/20160316006570/en/Micro-Prefab-Housing-Startup-KASITA-Revolutionizing-Attainable

While the home looks and feels high-end with sleek, modern, quality touches, Wilson says construction costs can be kept low because the units are designed to be mass produced. His hope is that this little house can be a solution for underserved communities—artists, creatives, immigrants, and young professionals—as the world's population continues to urbanize.

Chapter Seventeen
The Music House

From the outside, this home isn't weird at all. But looks can be deceiving. The fact that Ozzy Osbourne's gold album and other impressive music paraphernalia greet you at the front door might be your first clue that this home is truly something special.

Once inside, it's apparent where live music and special events producer Luis Zapata's passion lies. Rows of guitars line the living room, while upstairs there's a tribute to 80s bands. The media room is the envy of any avid record collector.

171

Where Music and Meditation Collide

But, wait: there are other motifs in this home. Water? Meditation? Many of these added touches are courtesy of Zapata's partner, makeup artist Mapy Ramos. It's her love for meditation that is apparent in the living room where guests are often surprised to find an altar for the practice perched under a "floating" fish tank.

And what goes well with fish? Shells! The couple is proud to show off their unique table encrusted with seashells, which Zapata rescued from a thrift store after considering how much time and energy the original owner appeared to have put into it.

While the front of the home is inconspicuous amid its suburban-like surroundings, the garage is another story.

"Visually, my favorite room was the garage, which holds a gorgeous piano and a make-up chair complete with movie star lights around a mirror," said *The Austinot's* Kelly McDonald when she visited the home while covering the Weird Homes Tour. "This space encompasses the loving cohabitation of the couple by providing a vibrant room for both of their passions. It even exhibits their Peruvian culture through an alpaca rug on the floor."[19]

19 McDonald, Kelli. "Exclusive Preview: Austin Weird Homes Tour 2015." *The Austinot*, May 12, 2015.
   http://austinot.com/weird-homes-tour-2015.

What's in the back? A chicken coop, of course. But there's a quail pen, too, and a Peruvian earth oven for cooking traditional pachamanca. Visitors to the home love conversing with Zapata and Ramos about their love of the neighborhood wildlife, their human neighbors, their baby goat neighbors, and the gorgeous creek that runs behind the home.

With all of these elements combined, it's no wonder the home is often called the "Peruvian Palace" of music.

CHAPTER EIGHTEEN
COMMUNITY FIRST! VILLAGE

Nestled in far East Austin is a strange development with a remarkable vision. The master-planned community is a development of Mobile Loaves & Fishes called Community First! Village. Its inhabitants? Men and women who are coming out of chronic homelessness.

Mobile Loaves & Fishes began when five parishioners of St. John Neumann Catholic Church in Austin took on the call to "Love your neighbor as yourself." Alan Graham and his friends began delivering meals out of the back of a minivan to men and women they found living on the streets of their city. Since those first few meals, Mobile Loaves & Fishes has served over 5 million more and, with the support of more than 18,000 volunteers, is now the largest prepared feeding program to the homeless and working poor in Austin.[20]

20 Mobile Loaves & Fishes. "What We Do."
    Accessed February 20, 2017.
    http://mlf.org/what-we-do/us/.

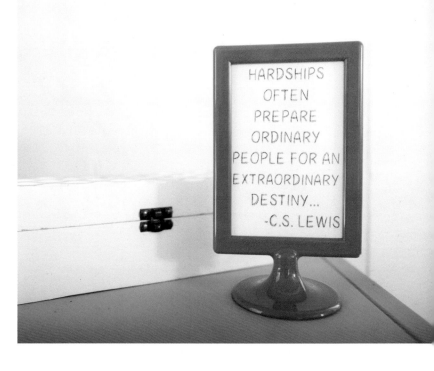

Once Graham and his friends tackled the problem of hunger, it was time to tackle another problem: shelter combined with community. That's how the organization's Community First! Village took shape.

Truly Inspired Housing

Community First! Village is a 27-acre master-planned community that provides affordable, permanent housing and a supportive community for the disabled, chronically homeless in Central Texas. Before you envision grey, cookie-cutter affordable houses lined up in neat rows, however, let's set the record straight. Community First! Village is truly helping to keep Austin's weird vibe alive. The housing options available to residents are as varied as the people living there. You'll find professionally designed micro-homes, RVs, canvas cottages, airstream trailers, and even tipis.

The community's amenities are truly one of a kind as well. The grounds include a memorial garden, columbarium, and prayer labyrinth, as well as an outdoor movie theater. There's a bed and breakfast for overnight visitors as well as a community market.

When we first included the village in our Weird Homes Tour, it was just getting off the ground. Now, it boasts 120 micro-homes, 100 RVs, and 20 canvas-sided cottages, and is likely to soon reach capacity, serving as home to 200 formerly homeless men and women.[21] A new medical facility for health screenings and other support services including hospice and respite care is now open to serve residents as well.

21 Mobile Loaves & Fishes. "Frequently Asked Questions." Accessed February 20, 2017. https://mlf.org/faqs/.

189

Chapter Nineteen
Florence's Comfort House

A bold, whimsical streak of color in the Montopolis neighborhood marks the place where Florence Ponziano lives. Now over 75 years old, Ponziano's spirit is timeless. And her home of more than twenty-five years, lovingly called "Florence's Comfort House," is a haven of love for neighbors young and old.

Ponziano has been called "the Mother Theresa of Montopolis," and for good reason. Her home is the center of a nonprofit mission to provide a place where kids are always welcome. Her passion is to help them live a better life—providing structure and a strong push towards education. She's turned a portion of her home into an open library where kids can sit and read donated books, or take them home to keep.

Light, Love, and Art

"The kids come to spend time and get away from the darkness in their own situations," explains Ponziano's nonprofit website, www.florencescom forthouse.org. "This darkness may be represented by a lack of food and care, the absence of someone to listen, or the danger present in a neighborhood frequented by drug dealers. Many times the people knocking on Flo's door are wonderful neighbors from low-income families who just need a boost. Flo provides love, laughter, and a protected space."[22]

22 Florence's Comfort House. "Flo's Story."
   Accessed February 20, 2017.
   http://www.florencescomforthouse.org/flos-story.html.

Part of the light and love Ponziano provides is the artwork that is present in and around her home. An artist at heart, she uses her creations to brighten the spirits of those who visit her home. She also uses her artwork to fund her programs and projects for children. Whether it's in her mosaics, wind chimes, bird houses, stained glass art, or her well-known art guitars, Ponziano's eye is always on color, light, and happiness.

Mixed in and among her artwork are creations by the children who spend time with her. Pottery, paintings, and other creations by precious little hands scattered around Montopolis's most colorful and caring home make it even more charming. Every corner of the home—both inside and out—is filled with a piece of art or memento with a story to tell.

Chapter Twenty

Houston Weird Homes Tour Sneak Peek

Austin may be the center of strange for Texas but it's certainly not the only haven of weird in the Lone Star State. When we contemplated other locations for the Weird Homes Tour, Houston was an obvious next stop. After all, the city has been host to the notoriously strange Houston Art Car Parade for more than thirty years, an event that has featured some of our own Austin Weird Homes Tour homeowners and art car enthusiasts.

And so, when we brought the Weird Homes Tour to Houston in October 2016, the city welcomed us with open arms. In fact, more homeowners signed up to be on our tour in Houston than ever before, and we were thrilled to give a portion of all ticket sales to Avenue CDC, which helps provide quality, affordable homes in the Washington Avenue community of Houston.

Hidden Art, Huge Spaces, and Hippos

So, what did we find in H-Town?

We found the homes of art collectors like Barbara Kimzey, who has an eye for discovering "Outsider Artists" (those with no formal art education) from places like Appalachia. We found the homes of artists like Bonnie Blue, an award-winning art car artist, folk, photo, and rock art creator. We found huge spaces like the home of Dawn Fudge, who lives in an 8,000-square-foot warehouse she bought from the Tejano band La Mafia; and the 5,000-square-foot, one-bedroom/art studio by Architect Scott Strasser, now the home of Beverley and Wayne Gilbert.

Oh, and then there's The Hippolotofus Home, filled with more than 2,000 pieces of hippo objects and hippo memorabilia (with a matching hippo art car, of course). No kidding.

We were graciously hosted by the Kiam Annex, the tenth oldest commercial building in Houston. Constructed in 1893, the second and third floors are the residence and studios of artists Jim Pirtle and Bronwyn Lauder, along with resident caretaker and magic-maker, Dawn Lerro. Ten thousand square feet are stuffed with objects left behind from the previous tenants including four clothing stores, a jewelry store, and a pawn shop, plus the art brought in by Pirtle from thirty-five years of object-making and collecting.

Our time in Houston has been spectacular. In fact, we should write a book about it. What do you think? Let us know!

Final Thoughts

Author O. Henry, one of Austin's original oddball inhabitants, once wrote, "The true adventurer goes forth aimless and uncalculating to meet and greet unknown fate."

It is this adventurous spirit that we discovered and have tried so tirelessly to capture with the Weird Homes Tour. Many of our homeowners have turned their living spaces into works of art or museums of fascination; not because it would bring them fame or riches—quite the contrary. They do it because it fulfills them on a personal level, often devoid of a desire to share it with the outside world at all. Many are without a grand plan or even a fleeting thought of, *What comes next?* And many know that there are certainly more practical ways to spend their time and resources.

It's to these homeowners we are immensely grateful. And it's for these homeowners we feel an obligation to help record and preserve what they've so passionately created. The Weird Homes Tour has been around for only a few short years and, in that time, a handful of the homes you've explored in these pages are already gone. Many were sold due to rising property taxes, an unfortunate byproduct of Austin's growing popularity. We're humbled to have had the opportunity to show off and capture images of these homes when we did. In the meantime, we're thrilled to have the opportunity to invest in the nonprofits working hard to make housing affordable and achievable in the areas they serve.

If you've enjoyed this tour through Austin's strangest homes, let us know. And if you know of other homes in Austin, around Texas, or in other parts of the country that would be perfect specimens for the Weird Homes Tour, please drop us a line, and follow us on Instagram @weirdhomestour. You can reach us at contact@weirdhomestour.com.

About the Authors

A shared love for interesting design, outsider art, eye-catching architecture, and all things weird and whimsical. These are the things that brought David J. Neff and Chelle Neff together and are the driving force catapulting their Weird Homes Tour™ into new markets each year.

By day, David is an author (*Weird Homes* is his third book) and eCommerce consultant, and Chelle owns and operates Urban Betty Salon, a Texas beauty-scene institution. The Weird Homes Tour has not only given the couple a way to satisfy their own curiosity about what lurks inside the county's weirdest homes, but it has also given them a way to give back to the communities that are home to these iconic treasures as each tour invests a percentage of its sales to local affordable housing nonprofits.

About Photographer Thanin Viriyaki

A picture is truly worth a thousand words. For this reason, we are grateful to Texas-based photographer Thanin Viriyaki for helping us write these stories through his lens and his unique perspective.

Viriyaki came from Bangkok, Thailand, at a very early age to settle in Texas and become an American. As a youth, he had lofty dreams of one day becoming a Transformer much like Optimus Prime but, due to his dreams being bigger than modern day scientific progress, his strong interest in art eventually led him to pick up a camera.

Viriyaki's mother would routinely ask "Do you really need to take so many pictures?" because of the numerous piles of photography covering his bedroom floor. The family camera became his tool to record inspirations for his drawings and paintings and eventually led him to take up photography for his major at the University of North Texas.